Milly, Mol... Beak...

"We may look different
but we feel the same."

At the bottom of the garden, in a pile of oak leaves, Milly and Molly found a big white duck's egg.

They tucked it up with Marmalade to keep it warm and waited for it to hatch.

Every morning they checked to see if it looked different.
And every night Milly's mum said, "maybe tomorrow."

The weeks went by and the duck's egg looked
no different.

Milly and Molly had almost given up hope
when, one morning, they heard the faintest
little chip, chip, chip.

As the chip, chip, chipping became more determined, the egg began to crack.

Milly and Molly watched very carefully as the little duckling gave one last heave and fell out of her shell.

She was yellow and soft and began to cheep.

Her little beak chipped at everything that
moved.
Milly and Molly called her Beaky.

Beaky washed in the bath

and slept in Marmalade's warm spot.

She ate puffed rice for breakfast

and worms for dinner.

Beaky went to school and ate the crumbs at lunchtime.

As Beaky grew older she changed colour and the mess she left behind got messier.

Milly's mum explained that it was time Beaky
went back under the oak tree where she had
come from.

Beaky understood. In fact, she liked it.
She found a friend to share her nest at

One day Beaky wouldn't go to breakfast.
She refused to leave her nest.

Milly's mum explained that Beaky was
hatching her own eggs and should not be
disturbed.

Beaky sat on her nest through wind

and rain.

Every morning Milly and Molly checked for progress. And every night Milly's mum said, "Maybe tomorrow."

Milly and Molly had almost given up hope when, one morning at breakfast, they heard a chip, chip, chipping. And there was Beaky chipping at the puffed rice with six little yellow Beakys of her own.